REMARKABLE
WILDLIFE
JOHN LESLEY
HIPPO
REDBACK
publishing

First Published 2026 by
Redback Publishing
Suite 6, 13a Narabang Way,
Belrose NSW 2085
Australia

www.redbackpublishing.com
orders@redbackpublishing.com

ISBN 978-1-761402-01-2

Author: John Lesley
Editor: Lucinda Dodds and Emma Dobinson
Designer: Redback Publishing

Original illustrations © Redback Publishing 2026
Originated by Redback Publishing

Acknowledgements
Abbreviations: l—left, r—right, b—bottom,
t—top, c—centre, m—middle
We would like to thank the following for permission to reproduce photographs (images © Shutterstock unless otherwise stated)

MIX
Paper from responsible sources
FSC™ C001507

A catalogue record for this book is available from the National Library of Australia

CONTENTS

WHAT IS A HIPPO?

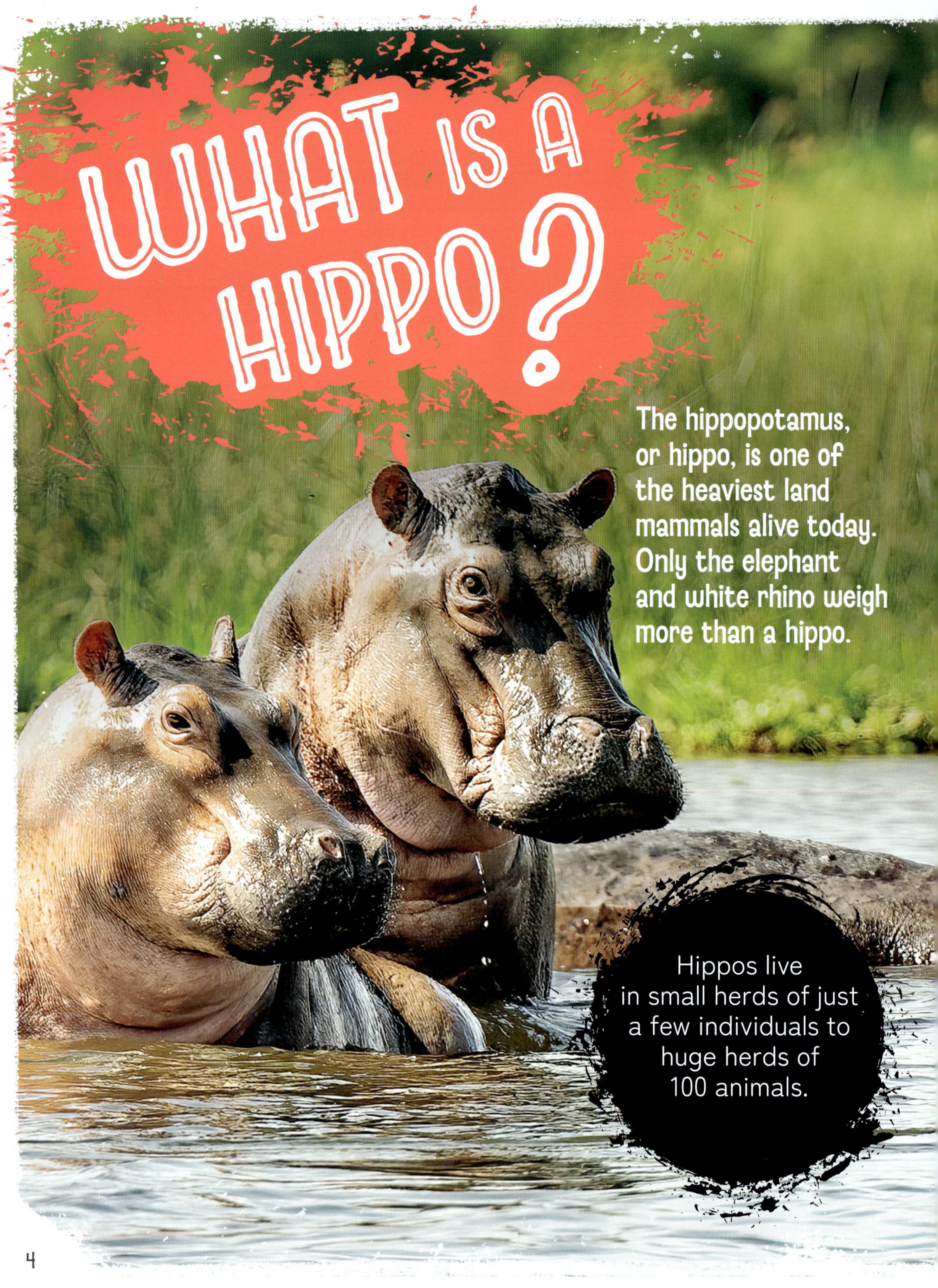

The hippopotamus, or hippo, is one of the heaviest land mammals alive today. Only the elephant and white rhino weigh more than a hippo.

Hippos live in small herds of just a few individuals to huge herds of 100 animals.

THERE ARE TWO SPECIES OF HIPPO ALIVE TODAY:

Nile hippo
Hippopotamus amphibius
Pygmy hippo
Choeropsis liberiensis

The hippo is a relative of dolphins and whales. All these animals had the same ancestors millions of years ago. Today, hippos are land animals, but they spend so much time in ponds, rivers and lakes that they are called semiaquatic.

The ancient Greeks called these animals 'river horses' and this is the origin of the name 'hippopotamus'. Hippos are not closely related to horses at all, and they don't look like them either!

HIPPO BASIC FACTS

HIPPO BODY

The hippo has a heavy body and thick legs. There is very little hair on its skin, which is a grey-brown colour.

BLOOD SWEAT

A hippo produces its own skin moisturiser called 'blood sweat', which acts like a sunscreen. This does not include any blood, but the chemicals in it make it appear red. Despite having a thick skin, hippos need to constantly look after their skin to stop it from cracking and getting infections. Blood sweat helps to keep the skin healthy, but hippos also cover themselves in mud to keep their skin from drying out.

SCIENTIFIC NAME:

Hippopotamus amphibius

OTHER NAMES:

Nile hippo,
common hippopotamus

TUSKS

Hippos have two large tusks that can grow to over 40 centimetres long. They use them for fighting and for defence against predators. The tusks are valuable on the black market, particularly since elephant ivory has become more difficult for poachers to obtain.

SIZE

WEIGHT: 2 tonnes for males, with females being lighter. As a comparison, a small car weighs about a tonne.

LENGTH: Hippos can grow to 5 metres long, not including the tail, and may have a height of 1.5 metres.

HIPPO ADAPTATIONS

UNDER THE WATER

A hippo's ears, nose and eyes are aligned at the top of the head. This allows the hippo to have most of its body under the water for long periods, while still breathing and being able to see what is happening on the land and the surface around it.

Hippos can also stay under the water by closing their noses and surviving on the air already in their lungs. They actually walk on the bottom of rivers and lakes.

The hippo is a very heavy animal. Resting in water reduces the stress on the hippo's legs and feet, and keeps its body cool under the hot, African sunshine.

OPEN MOUTH

A hippo can open its mouth to over 150°, so wide that the upper and lower jaws almost form a straight line. Hippos are one of very few animals that are capable of doing this. They use the open gape as a threat display to other hippos or any animal that they want to warn to stay away.

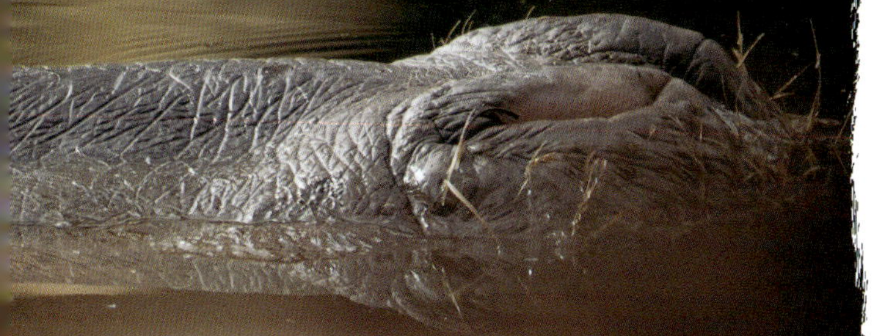

SPLASHING

Hippos splash in the water as a threat display and a warning not to intrude on their territory.

WEBBED TOES

Hippos have webbed toes that help them move around in the water.

DEFENCE AND ATTACK

Because of their weight, hippos do not normally move quickly. Because they appear to be so slow-moving, this encourages people to think it is safe to go near them in the wild, either on land or in the water. In fact, if it feels threatened, a hippo can use a short burst of speed to charge at an intruder in its territory. When two tonnes of hippo attack, the results can be lethal. They also use their teeth and long tusks as weapons.

HIPPO HABITAT

Pygmy hippo

AFRICA

Hippos live in sub-Saharan Africa, south of the Sahara Desert. They need habitats where there is plenty of grass to eat, and where the water sources are deep enough for them to remain completely under the water. Because of this, hippos seek territories where there are rivers, lakes or swamps.

ANGRY HIPPOS

Hippos are very territorial and easily angered if people or other animals come too close to a lake or pond that they have claimed as their own. Hippos need to submerge themselves in water during the day, when the heat from the sun would damage their skins and cause them to overheat. They cannot sweat to cool down, so they stay in water instead.

Because water is so necessary for their health, hippos guard their own water source and its surroundings aggressively. They are less likely to be angered when they are roaming grasslands and browsing on grass. Despite this, a hippo can be a dangerous animal in any location.

Hippos leave large amounts of droppings in water. This provides nutrients that help aquatic plants to grow.

Wild hippos live in Africa, but once inhabited Europe and Asia too!

HIPPO LIFE CYCLE

CALVES

Eight months after mating, the female gives birth, often underwater, to one calf. She feeds it on milk until it is old enough to graze on grass. When the calf is in the water, the mother hippo needs to push it up to the surface so it can take breaths regularly. She may also allow the baby to ride on her back.

Females give birth in a secluded spot to keep the calf safe. If the dominant male in the herd finds a newborn calf, he may kill it. Males are intent on protecting their watery territory from any intruders, even newborn hippos.

HERDS

Hippos live in herds led by one dominant male called a bull. The female is called a cow, and the baby is a calf. The male hippo claims a territory in the water and shares it with the rest of the herd, which includes cows, younger males and calves.

LIFESPAN

Hippos can live for 50 years in zoos, where they are spared the stresses of life in the wild. In their natural habitat, they live for about 40 years.

A newborn hippo calf may weigh about 30 kg.

Hippos live in family groups called herds or pods.

WHAT HIPPOS EAT

Although hippos spend so much time in water, aquatic plants are not a large part of their diet.

FARMS

In their constant search for food, hippos will sometimes eat crops, causing conflicts with farmers.

GRASS

Nile hippos are herbivores and usually eat only grass. They spend most of the day in water if they can and then may move out onto land at night to graze on grass. Avoiding too much sun on their skin is a major factor affecting when and where hippos eat. Overcast and cool days are perfect times for hippos to leave the water and graze during the day.

WANDERING

They wander long distances during the evening looking for grass to eat but need to return to water to escape the burning sun during the day. Being so heavy means that they need to consume a lot of grass each day. Hippos make trails through grasslands and use these to get to places where they know there is food.

HIPPOS AND PEOPLE

HUNTING HIPPOS

Throughout thousands of years of human history, people have hunted hippos for food and even for sport. Cave art in various parts of Europe shows that hippos were hunted there in the distant past, although no hippos live in Europe now.

Hippos are currently being killed by poachers for food, to sell body parts, and in particular for the ivory of their tusks.

DEADLY

Hippos may be the deadliest animals in the world, apart from the billions of disease-carrying insects. Hundreds of people are killed each year by wild hippos charging at them or attacking them in water.

ANGRY HIPPOS

Wild hippos are aggressive towards humans who enter their territory. Hippos are very territorial and do not tolerate any intrusion into an area they consider to be their own. A hippo can run at a human and easily knock them over, trample, bite or kill them. Humans in boats are not safe, as hippos can tip boats over and attack the occupants when they fall into the water.

A hippo can run at over 40 km/h for a short distance, so you would not be able to outrun one if it was chasing you!

HIPPOS IN ZOOS

In the past, hippos in zoos were often kept in cramped and unnatural conditions, with no access to deep water.

Modern zoos provide water tanks where their hippos can spend time. Underwater viewing of hippos walking around on the bottom of the tank is achieved by using thick glass as one of the tank walls.

Having a large herd of hippos, as occurs in the wild, is not possible in a zoo. A male and female may be the only two hippos on display.

Zoos around the world are mostly very conscious of their responsibility to conserve the hippos in their collections.

Hippos can become tame in zoos, but they remain dangerous, wild animals.

MEGAFAUNA

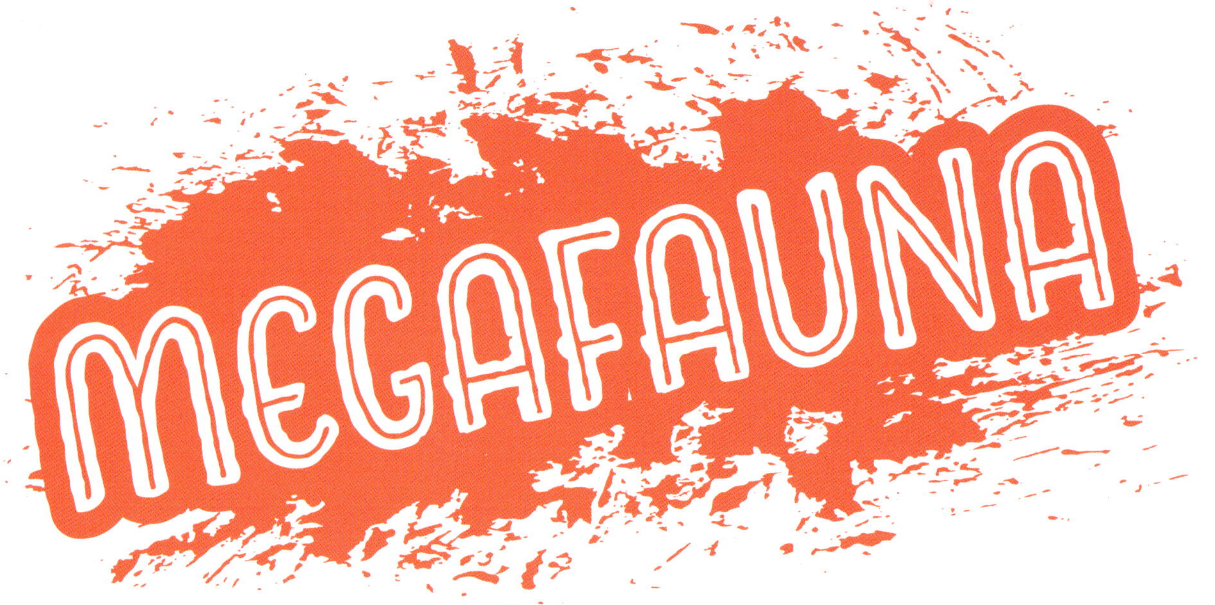

ANCIENT MEGAFAUNA

The ancient megafauna, which included mammoths and gigantic sharks, mostly became extinct thousands of years ago. Some megafauna did survive that mass extinction, and hippos are one of the animals that managed to make it to the present.

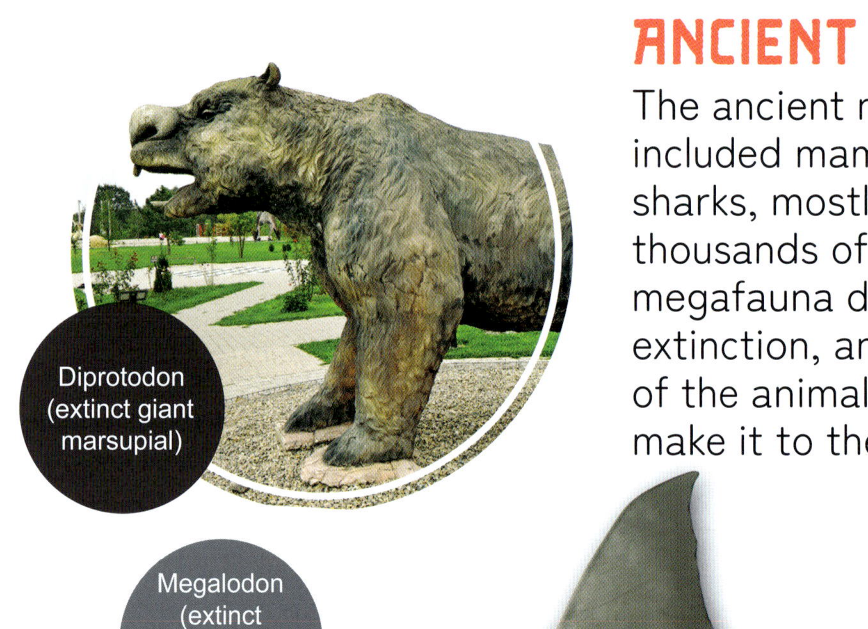

Diprotodon (extinct giant marsupial)

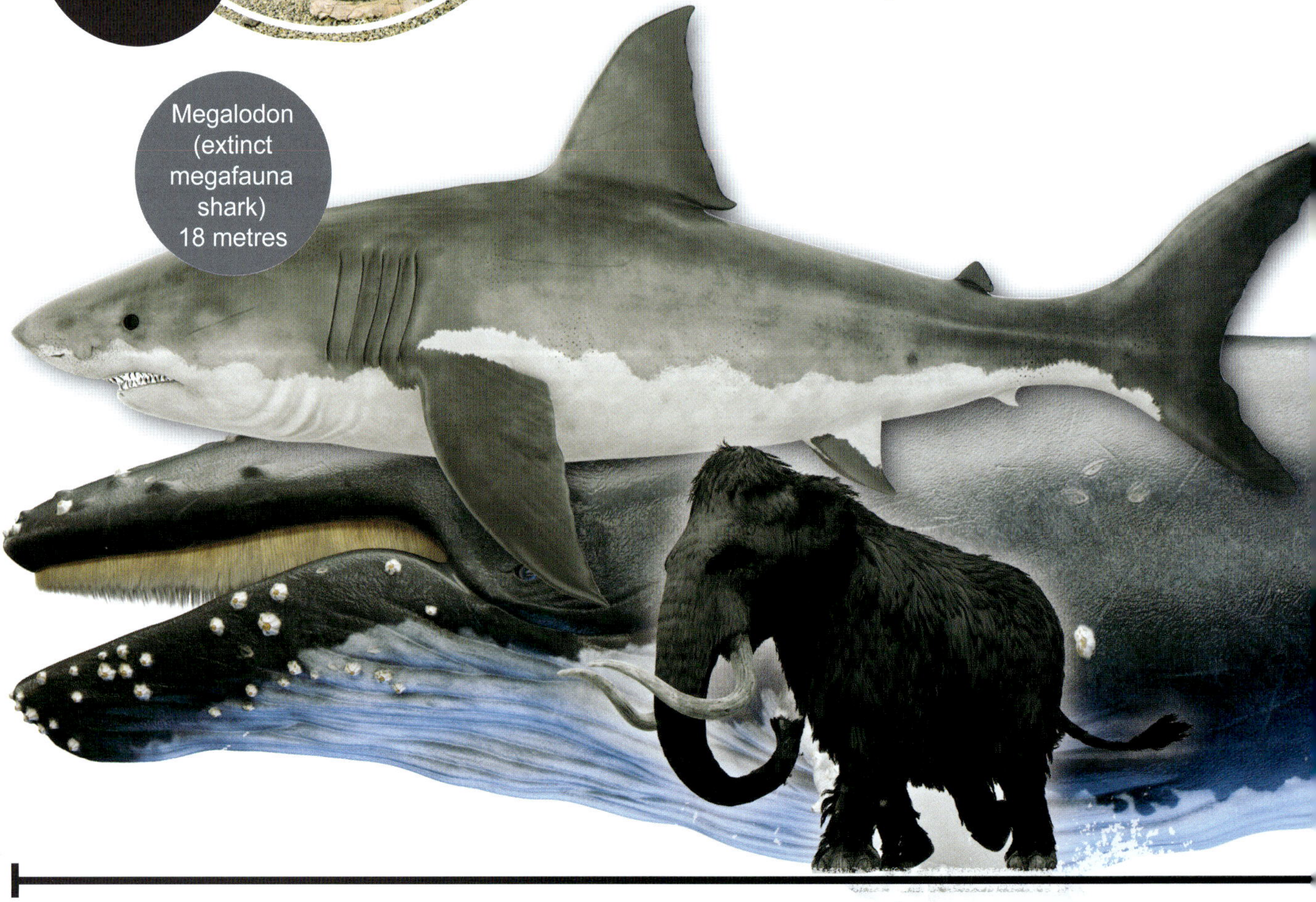

Megalodon (extinct megafauna shark) 18 metres

EXTINCTION

The past extinction of the megafauna was probably due to a combination of natural climate change and perhaps hunting by early humans. Today, hippos and other surviving land megafauna are suffering a major loss of habitat due to increasing land use by people. Modern climate change is affecting rainfall and temperature, making the food sources of megafauna less secure. Add to this the effect of poaching, and the future of the world's last megafauna becomes very uncertain.

MODERN MEGAFAUNA

The world still has living megafauna, including hippos, elephants, giraffes, whales and rhinos. Their large size and special needs for survival are placing them all at risk of decline in numbers or even extinction.

Blue whale 33 metres

Hippo 5 metres

5m

33m

THREATS TO HIPPOS

LIONS

Lions will attempt to attack hippo calves, but if a hippo retreats into the water, the lion will usually give up the chase. A large, healthy hippo is a difficult and dangerous animal for a group of lions to kill.

Lions prefer to wait until they can find a sick or old hippo before they attack.

CROCODILES

Hippos and crocodiles share the same habitat, so interactions between the two are frequent and violent. Hippos will kill crocodiles that try to attack them, but some crocodiles manage to kill calves and sick or injured adult hippos.

HUMANS

Humans also hunt hippos, but our main effect on hippo numbers is through taking their habitat for buildings and farms.

FARMERS AND FISHERS

In search of food, hippos may take crops and come into conflict with farmers as a result. People fishing in lakes and ponds are also likely to have to confront an angry hippo who thinks he owns that waterway and is ready to defend it from any intruder.

GAME RESERVES

Game tourism is an important way that the conservation of wild animals is funded.

Game parks and reserves in Africa include a mix of private and government-owned areas.

Nearly all of the Nile hippos alive today live in reserves and game parks in Africa. Conservation officers have a constant battle to keep poachers away and stop them killing hippos and other animals on the reserves.

Poachers use advanced techniques to hunt animals in reserves, and conservation officers need to keep up with their own technology to try to stop them.

PYGMY HIPPO

Choeropsis liberiensis

DUNG FLINGING

Male pygmy hippos spread their droppings around by flicking it with their tail. This is the same habit that male Nile hippos have. It is a good way of communicating with other hippos in the area and letting them know that the territory they are in is already taken.

SIZE

At a height of only one metre and with a weight of about 200 kilograms, pygmy hippos are not as dangerous and aggressive as Nile hippos. They live in smaller herds, or even alone, and the males are not as ready to fight with each other over territories. Despite this, they have long, pointed tusks that they can use if an animal or a person is a threat.

HABITAT AND DIET

Pygmy hippos only live in the western parts of sub-Saharan Africa. Unlike their huge relatives, these little hippos prefer forests where they can hide from predators. They come out to feed at night, when it is more difficult for predators to see them. They like to eat plants and fruits, and only a small amount of grass, unlike the Nile hippos that live mainly on grass. Both types of hippos share the need to spend long periods of time in water.

IS IT EXTINCT?

The actual number of pygmy hippos left in the wild is not known for certain, but it could already be close to extinction in its natural habitat. This makes the zoo populations of pygmy hippos very precious.

THREATS

Pygmy hippos are hunted by other wild animals, such as leopards. People also kill them for food. Hunting and the loss of natural forests and clean waterways have all contributed to decreasing numbers of pygmy hippos.

WAR

During war, when people are displaced and their crops destroyed during the conflict, they sometimes turn to bushmeat for food. Bushmeat is a term for meat from wild animals, including hippos.

SORTING ANIMALS INTO GROUPS

Biologists divide all living things around the world into groups. They call this process classification.

ANIMALS ARE CLASSIFIED INTO TWO MAIN GROUPS:

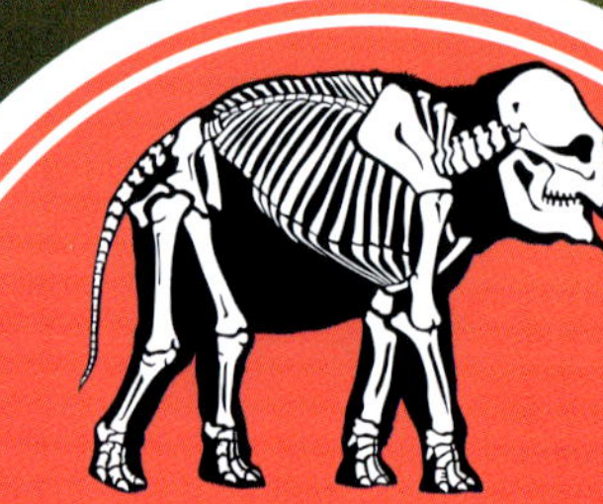

VERTEBRATES

Vertebrates have a backbone

INVERTEBRATES

Invertebrates do not have a backbone

Vertebrates are further divided into five groups called classes:
MAMMALS (Mammalia)
BIRDS (Aves)
REPTILES (Reptilia)
AMPHIBIANS (Amphibia)
FISH
Humans are in the class called Mammalia. Hippos are mammals and also belong in the class called Mammalia.

ENDANGERED HIPPOS

RED LIST

The International Union for Conservation of Nature (IUCN) Red List is a catalogue of the state of conservation of living things around the world.

The Red List considers the large Nile hippos to be Endangered. There are possibly only about 130,000 Nile hippos left in the wild across all of Africa. The pygmy hippo is close to extinction and numbers left in the wild are very low.

Pygmy hippo

GLOSSARY

black market	illegal trade in animals and their body parts
bushmeat	meat from wild animals in Africa
conservation officer	person in charge of guarding animals in reserves
herbivore	animal that eats mainly plants as food
poacher	person who kills or takes animals illegally from the wild
secluded	hidden
semiaquatic	spending part of the time in water
submerge	place under the water
territory	area that an animal claims as its own
tusk	long, sharp tooth

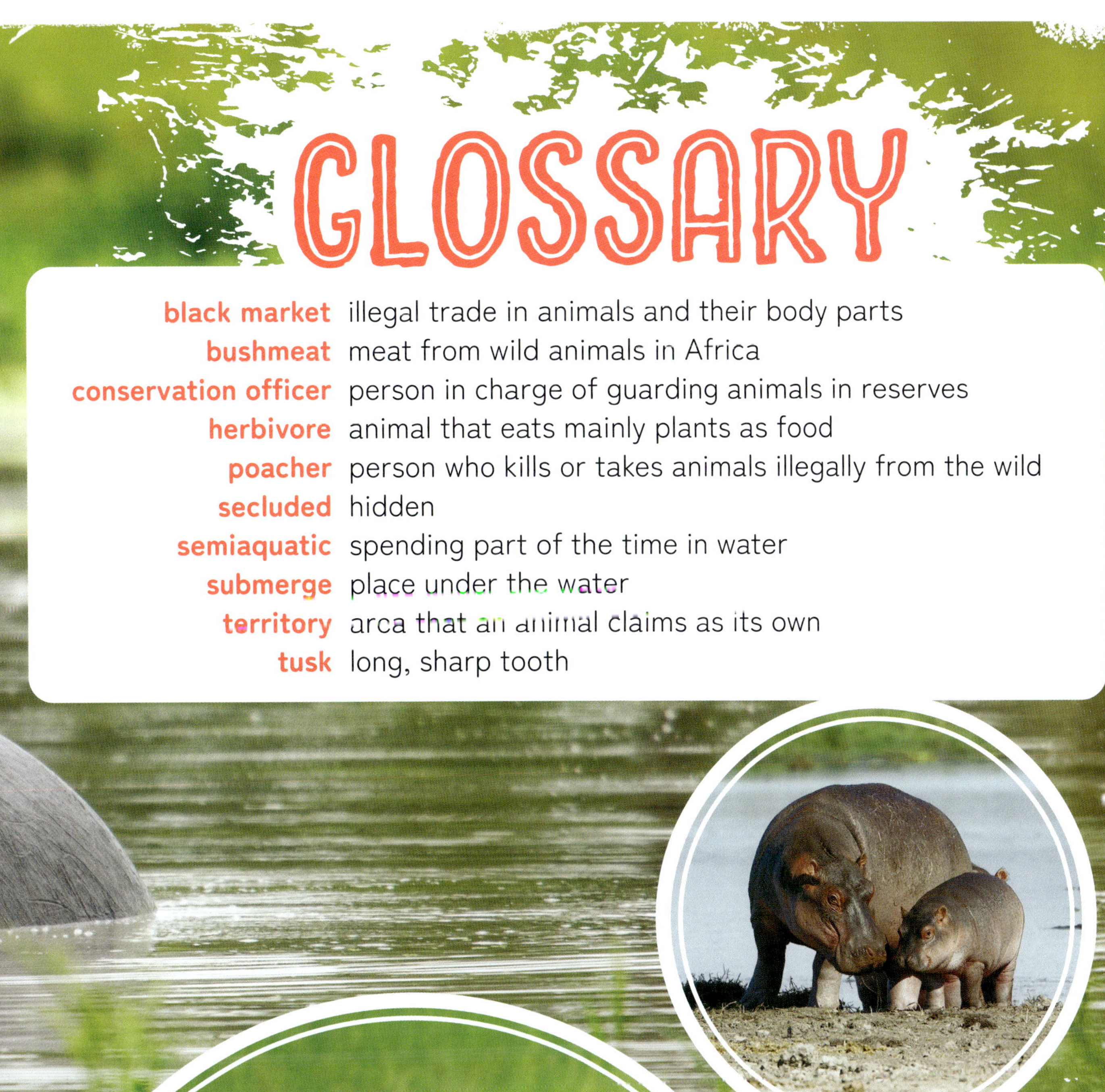

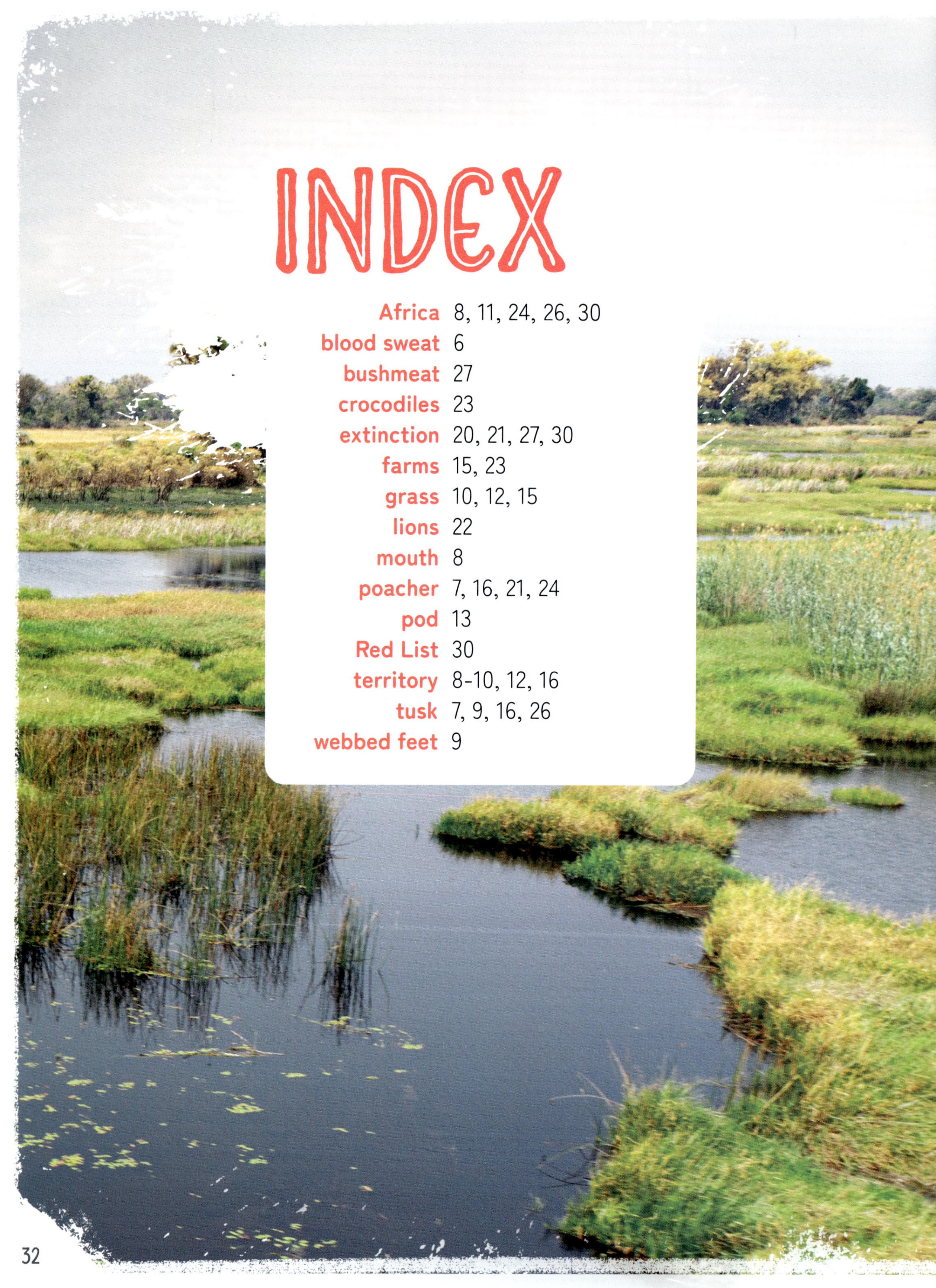

INDEX